CORNWALL FROM ABOVE

JOHN SUCH

with an introduction by
Liz Luck

Alison Hodge

St Germans

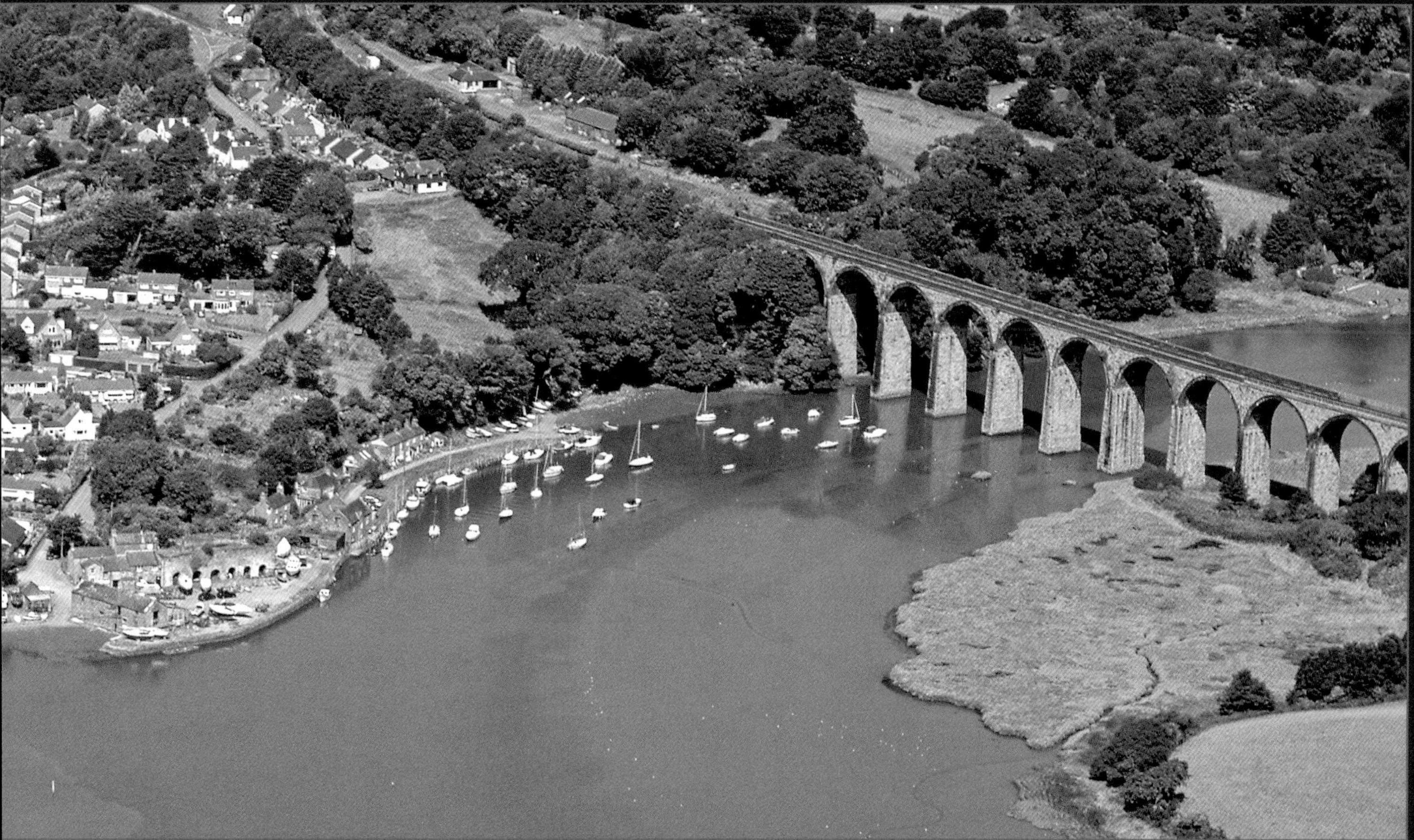

Glendurgan

Foreword

I was born in 1966 in Newquay, Cornwall, and had a great childhood growing up living by the sea. From the age of 12 I knew I was going to be a photographer. The first photograph I ever took was of a spider's web, on an Anny 120 camera, and I remember being so excited as to how the picture would look once it had been developed and printed.

I then began to take lots of photographs of just about anything I found interesting, and realized that photography is about capturing the moment – anything from a sunset to a smile – making it last forever. I started reading every book and magazine I could find on the subject. It became quite an obsession.

My first bit of luck happened when I was at comprehensive school, and I discovered that there was a two-year photography course for students in Year 10. As soon as the course began, I couldn't get enough, and after each lesson I would stay on and go through morning as well as dinner break. This gave me an early understanding of photography which was to be invaluable.

The transition from that course to where I am now has been a long and winding road, involving me in many styles of photography, including educational, social, PR and freelance, and it has taken time to build up a portfolio of clients and contacts. The very first time I took an aerial photograph – in the year 2000 – took me right back to when I was 12 years old – reliving the excitement, and knowing this was going to become an important part of my life.

I realized I had an 'eye' for photography from the air and, just as important, I knew how to get the right shots, by telling the pilot where I wanted him to position the plane to enable me to get the optimum photograph. Timing is just as important, and my philosophy has been that if it does not look right in the view finder, then it will be the same when the film is processed, so communication with the pilot about the kind of shot I am after is essential.

I have now been involved in photography for over 20 years. I still love taking photographs, and I find it extremely rewarding seeing my work published in books, brochures and magazines. Looking at my aerial photographs, I realized I had some unique images of Cornwall, which in themselves would make a great book. And so *Cornwall from Above* was born.

I hope these images give you as much pleasure as I have had in taking them.

John Such, 2006

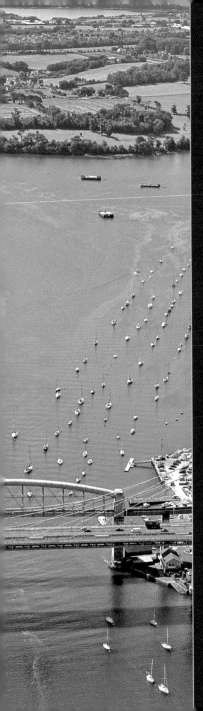

Introduction

Why does Cornwall feel different? Why does my heart lurch and lift every time I cross the Tamar heading west; or at the sight of Carn Brea rising in silhouette above Redruth rugby ground, or the sun going down over Clay Country; or when a hush falls in a pub as someone sings *Lower Lights*? Is it just because it's home, the place of my birth? If so, would I feel the same way heading home if I lived in a lovely village in Dorset or a great city of the north?

Perhaps it is just the sentiment of belonging, being part of a compact geographical unit, feeling a sense of kinship with other people so caught. But there's more to Cornwall, isn't there? I often wonder if the word 'Cornwall' also resonates (with that deep, familiar note) for other people in Britain, or beyond, in the way it does for the Cornish. When someone in Stevenage or Shropshire sees one of those atmospheric advertisements in a magazine, designed to entice them here on holiday, or hears a victorious sportsman making a point of saying that they come from Cornwall, or an artist recalling the influence that Cornwall has had upon them, do they think, 'Ah yes, Cornwall. I know what Cornwall means to me.'? Does it conjure up an immediate and clear national identity in their mind, as would Scotland, say, or Spain, or would it have for them no more powerful a character than any other of England's beautiful counties?

Leaving aside the emotion – the love and the pride – it is still possible to identify and rationalize the sense of difference that Cornish people feel about Cornwall. You can pick out its curious elements, echoes of which may have settled in the memories of people far away, people who have never been here.

It has a different history: you can feel it even if you know nothing of Cornwall's Celtic past, its ancient sea links with Mediterranean civilizations, its sense of separateness from England, and its long resistance to Roman and Anglo-Saxon (and later) influences from over the Tamar. There are plenty of clues to be found today in the clearly un-English place-names on every map and signpost; the mysterious saints that gave their names to isolated churches; the cramped patterns of fields and hedges and lanes, stone circles, crosses and megalithic tombs; the black and white flag flying above public buildings.

Cornwall has its own language: not a quaint confection to amuse visitors, but something manifestly older and harsher than you might expect. You only have to hear it spoken or see it written to know that this is the tongue of a deeply foreign country, a place with a different story to tell. Only the Welsh or the Bretons might find it familiar.

Its geographical position makes it special: sticking out into the Atlantic like a witch's finger, Cornwall is nearly an island, and everything, everywhere, is affected by the sea. Up on Bodmin Moor you might be in the middle of the county, but you can see slivers of light on both coasts. Even when you can't actually see the sea, when you're down in a hollow or a deep, dank lane somewhere, you can still sense it nearby, smell its salt in the air: it lightens the sky and it stiffens the wind and the spirit. And when you're in what seems to be an inland town or village – Truro, say, or Tresillian, Polbathic, Calstock, Wadebridge or Lostwithiel – the sea creeps in to meet you twice a day, slowly surging deep into the remote and crumpled folds of the countryside through a network of drowned river valleys. So Cornish people have always looked to the sea naturally, unconsciously: for their livelihoods, for their sustenance, for their connection with the outside world.

It has a hard and rocky heart: Cornwall's complex geology is at the root of everything; it explains and forms the beloved landscape. Its bare bones are always close to the surface. The serpentine of the Lizard, the slates of Tintagel, and above all the great granite spine of the moors, its fringes suffused with minerals, all help to give Cornwall its shape, its bearing, its wondrously contrasting landscapes, its character, its agriculture, its vegetation and its historic wealth.

And then there is the weather: unreliable, capricious, and impossible to read. Although the climate is generally mild and damp, with tender tropical plants flourishing in the open in lush and verdant gardens, we all know that the weather can turn on a sixpence. It's like standing on the prow of a ship and seeing the fronts come in: whatever the weather, we get it first and it passes quickly. It means we don't get bogged down; it sculpts the trees and it keeps us on our toes.

Successive mining depressions in the nineteenth and early twentieth centuries drove hundreds of thousands of Cornish miners and their families to leave their homeland to search for work in silver, gold and copper mines all over the world. With them they took not only their skills under ground, but also their Cornish way of life, their sense of difference, their national pride: tea treats, mine picnics and Cornish wrestling, silver bands and Wesleyan hymns. Today, in settlements from California to Brazil to Australia there are families called Hosken, Blamey and Penrose, Bray, Rule and Skewes still baking pasties and saffron buns, and thinking of Camborne as home.

Cornwall's identity is so strong that it can survive any amount of exportation and dilution. Cornwall feels different simply because it is.

Kernow Bys Vyken.

Liz Luck. January 2006

7

Brunel's Royal Albert Bridge and viaduct, and the Tamar Suspension Bridge

Mudflats

Gwennap Pit

Restormel Castle

Antony House

Talskiddy

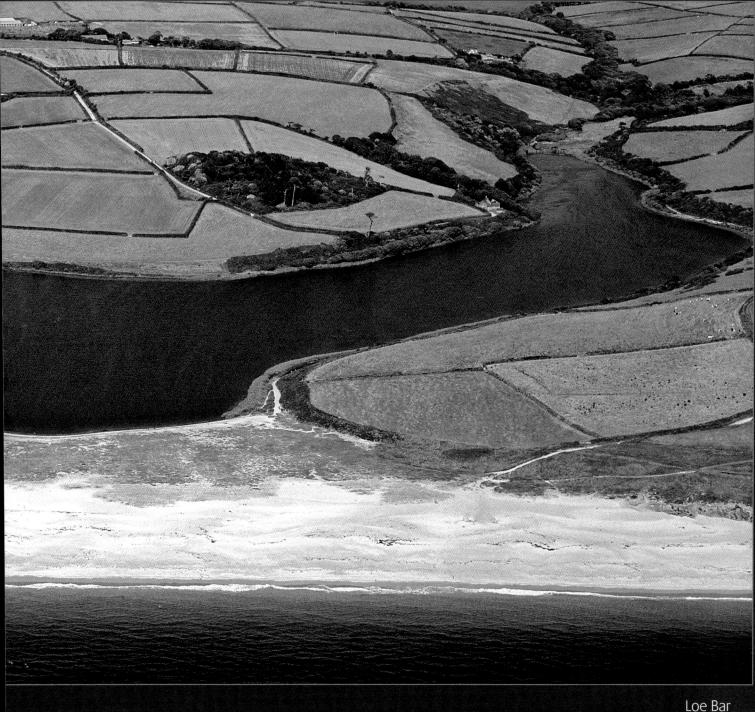

Loe Bar

St Ives

St Mawes

Port Isaac

Mevagissey

Mousehole

Charlestown

Trevose Lighthouse

Godrevy Lighthouse

Pendeen Lighthouse

Lizard Lifeboat station

Padstow Lifeboat house and boat ramp

Shipwreck near Land's End

Geevor Tin Mine

35

China clay workings

China clay workings

Clay settling tanks

Wheal Jane tailings dam

The Eden Project

Kynance Cove

St Michael's Mount

Chapel Point

Polzeath

Gribbin Head

Fowey

Newquay

St Mawes and St Anthony Head

Trelissick

Pendennis Point and Falmouth Docks

Nare Head and Gull Rock

Fields near Zennor

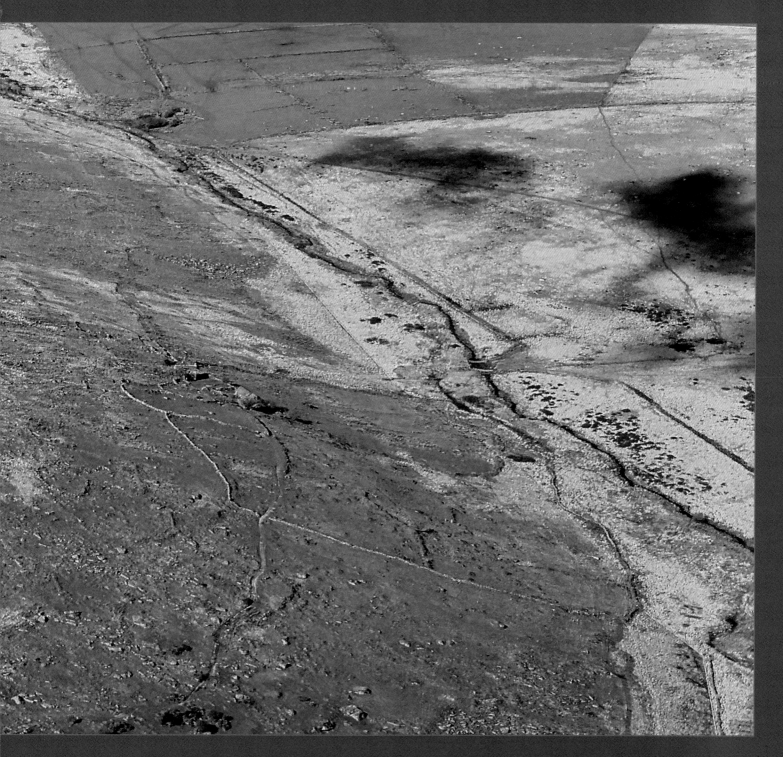

Brown Willy, Bodmin Moor

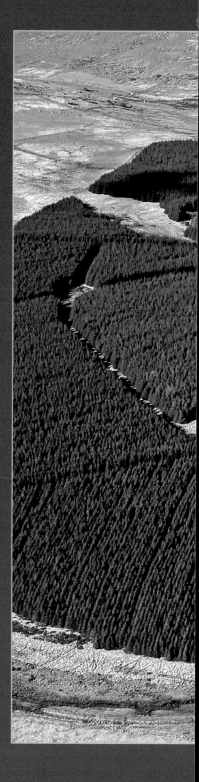

Wooded valley on the edge of Bodmin Moor

Conifer plantation, Bodmin Moor

Cape Cornwall

Camel estuary

Notes on the photographs

PAGES 2–3: **St Germans**, on the River Tiddy – part of the Lynher estuary, which joins the Tamar downriver from Saltash.

PAGE 4: A wooded valley drops steeply to the hamlet of Durgan, on the Helford estuary. **Glendurgan** – one of Cornwall's famous, subtropical valley gardens – flourishes in the warm microclimate.

PAGES 8–9: The Tamar forms a natural border between Devon and Cornwall. The **Royal Albert Bridge**, designed by Isambard Kingdom Brunel, and opened in 1859, is one of his greatest railway achievements. The **Tamar Suspension Bridge**, opened in 1961, was at that time the longest suspension bridge in the UK. In 2001, it became the first suspension bridge in the world to be widened using cantilevers.

PAGES 10–11: **Mudflats** on the Lynher River, south of Saltash.

PAGE 12: Between Redruth and Penryn, **Gwennap Pit** is 35 metres in diameter, 110 metres in circumference, and 6 metres deep. In the 18th century, it attracted thousands to hear the Methodist preacher John Wesley. It is thought that the pit originated in a depression caused by the ground collapsing into an abandoned mine below. It assumed its present form in 1806.

PAGE 13: Perched on high ground, and surrounded by a deep moat, **Restormel Castle**, near Lostwithiel, dates from c. 1100. It was once home to Edward, the Black Prince.

PAGE 14: On the Antony peninsula, south of Saltash, **Antony House** dates from the 18th century. The extensive parkland was landscaped by Humphry Repton.

PAGE 15: The hamlet of **Talskiddy**, near St Columb Major.

PAGES 16–17: A wide bank of shingle, **Loe Bar** separates Loe Pool – the largest freshwater lake in Cornwall, into which flows the River Cober – from the sea. Scene of many shipwrecks, the Bar, west of Helston, is home to much wildlife and rare plants.

PAGES 18–19: **St Ives** grew prosperous on its fishing industry, and from the 19th century attracted artists and photographers. The fish declined, and the coming of the railway brought Victorian holiday-makers. With its crystal blue waters, surf and white sand, St Ives is now one of Cornwall's most famous holiday towns.

PAGE 20: The sheltered location of **St Mawes**, on the Fal estuary, provides safe anchorage for small boats and yachts. Originally a fishing village, St Mawes is now an up-market holiday resort.

PAGE 21: Located at the mouth of a stream in a deep valley on the inhospitable north Cornish coast, the sheltered harbour of **Port Isaac** exported stone, ores, limestone and salt. The coming of larger ships, the railway, and the motor lorry ended this trade, and Port Isaac is now a holiday village.

PAGES 22–23: Unlike many coastal villages in Cornwall, **Mevagissey** is still a working harbour, employing fishermen who ply their trade in small boats – trawling, netting, long-lining and hand-lining.

PAGE 24: West of Penzance, on the Mount's Bay coast, **Mousehole** has an almost circular harbour, protected from winter gales by sturdy wooden beams across the harbour entrance. Fishing from the harbour has almost died out, but Mousehole is still largely unspoilt, and is one of Cornwall's prettiest coastal villages.

PAGE 25: A Georgian 'new town', the port of **Charlestown** was built by local landowner Charles Rashleigh, to export copper and china clay. Today it is home to many old ships used in the film industry.

PAGE 26: The first oil light was lit on the high granite cliffs at **Trevose Head** in 1847, to guide ships in the Bristol Channel. The light was electrified in 1974, and automated in 1995. The tower is 27 metres high.

PAGE 27: Immortalized by Virginia Woolf in her novel *To the Lighthouse*, **Godrevy Lighthouse** is situated in St Ives Bay. The 26-metre tower was built in 1859, and the light was automated in 1939. In 1995 it was converted to solar power.

PAGE 28: Built on a flattened headland at Pendeen Watch, **Pendeen Lighthouse** and fog signal were commissioned in 1900. The tower is 17 metres high, and the light was automated in 1995.

PAGE 29: The **Lizard Lifeboat station**, built in 1914, served until 1961, when it was replaced by a new boathouse.

PAGES 30–31: The **Padstow Lifeboat station**, down 127 steep steps at Mother Ivey's Bay, Trevose Head, has a 73-metre slipway. Malcolm Arnold's *Padstow Lifeboat March* marked the building of this boathouse in 1967. A new boathouse is now being built.

PAGES 32–33: There are over 3,000 wrecks around the Cornish coast. The 1,846-tonne RMS *Mulheim*, ran on to rocks near Land's End in 2003, with its 2,200-tonne cargo of waste plastic.

PAGES 34–35: The closure of **Geevor Tin Mine** in 1990 ended some 2,000 years of tin-mining in west Cornwall. The workings extended one mile out under the sea, and reached a depth of 640 metres. Geevor is now the largest preserved mining site in the UK.

PAGES 36–37: A pyramid-shaped 'burrow' of waste material, and a disused, water-filled pit – part of the **china clay workings** near

Carclaze, St Austell. Cornish china clay is of the highest quality, and demand exceeds supply.

PAGES 38–39: Some of the **old clay pits** are 90 metres deep and up to a mile in circumference. China clay is obtained from open pits by powerful jets of water that wash everything in their path to the bottom of the pit. Repeated washings separate the clay from the waste.

PAGE 40: On the surface, the clay passes to **settling tanks** and, after the removal of all impurities, to the 'dry'.

PAGE 41: Metal-rich drainage water in the tailings dam at **Wheal Jane**, once an important mine in the Carnon Valley, south-west of Truro, which produced tin, zinc, copper and silver.

PAGES 42–43: The Eden Project – a Millennium project to mark the year 2000 – is located in a former china clay pit at Bodelva, near St Austell. Two vast biomes, like giant bubbles, house plants from the humid tropics and warm temperate regions of the world.

PAGES 44–45: White sand, turquoise water, and multi-coloured serpentine rock characterize **Kynance Cove**, near Lizard Point.

PAGE 46: One of England's most famous landmarks, **St Michael's Mount**, near Penzance, is a rocky island, with medieval castle and church, approached at low tide via a cobbled causeway.

PAGE 47: The South West Coast Path runs along the clifftop past **Chapel Point**, south of Mevagissey.

PAGE 48: A favourite place of poet Sir John Betjeman, **Polzeath** is one of the best surfing beaches in North Cornwall.

PAGE 49: Jutting into St Austell Bay, **Gribbin Head** is marked by the red-and-white striped Daymark Tower, erected in 1832 to distinguish this headland for shipping from St Anthony Head, near Falmouth.

PAGE 50: Across the harbour from Fowey, the old boat-building village of **Polruan** clings to the hillside at the mouth of the River Fowey.

PAGE 51: A sheltered, deep-water port, **Fowey** exported tin and china clay all over the world. Drake, Raleigh and Frobisher all sailed from here, and Fowey is now a popular harbour for all kinds of sailing craft.

PAGES 52–53: The sheltered beaches of Towan, Great Western and Tolcarne at **Newquay**, Cornwall's most popular holiday destination, and the UK surf capital.

PAGES 54–55: Newquay, formerly a busy fishing port, now a lively resort.

PAGES 56–57: Rock, on the Camel estuary, is a major watersports centre, with long stretches of sandy beaches.

PAGES 58–59: Looking across **St Mawes** and the Percuil River to **St Anthony Head**. The Tudor St Mawes Castle, on the far right of the photograph, guards the eastern side of Carrick Roads, while St Anthony's Lighthouse guides ships clear of the Manacles rocks.

PAGES 60–61: The **Trelissick** estate slopes down to the tidal creeks of the Fal estuary. The parkland was largely laid out in the early 19th century, with a fortune made from tin-mining. Trelissick Garden contains a collection of tender and exotic plants.

PAGES 62–63: Built by Henry VIII as part of a chain of fortresses on the southern coast of England, **Pendennis Castle** guards the western side of Carrick Roads. Falmouth is the third largest natural harbour in the world, and Cornwall's premier port. It has been the start or finish point for record-breaking round-the-world voyages. **Falmouth Docks** offer a thriving ship repair yard, bunkering facilities, cargo handling and yacht building.

PAGES 64–65: Sea mist, **Nare Head and Gull Rock**, on the Roseland peninsula. Gull Rock (given to the National Trust in 1989 by Michael Trinick to mark his year as High Sheriff of Cornwall) is one of the largest seabird breeding areas on the south coast of England.

PAGES 66–67: A patchwork of ancient, granite-hedged fields stretches to the clifftop near Zennor.

PAGES 68–69: The high ground of **Bodmin Moor** is dominated by tors and granite-strewn slopes, and the remains of ancient farming systems.

PAGES 70–71: Brown Willy, Bodmin Moor, looking across to Cold Northcott wind farm. At 420 metres, Brown Willy is the highest point in Cornwall. The wind turbines were erected in 1993.

PAGE 72: A **wooded valley** on the edge of Bodmin Moor.

PAGE 73: A commercial **conifer plantation** on Bodmin Moor.

PAGES 74–75: Four miles north of Land's End is **Cape Cornwall**, England's only cape. The brick stack is the remains of a 19th-century mine.

PAGES 76–77: Sunset on the **Camel estuary**, near Padstow.

Acknowledgements

I should like to thank a number of people who have assisted me professionally, and who have helped to make this book a reality: Keith Appleby, my photography tutor from 1981 to 1983; Steve and Karen Windle from ScanAir UK; Captain and all the other pilots I have flown with over the years; Richard Elwell and David Wheaton, who are responsible for all my corporate design; Steve Hicks at AO Printworks for all those scans; and Samantha Mason at Bubble PR. I am grateful to Liz Luck and The National Trust for their essential contributions to *Cornwall from Above*, and I would like to thank Alison Hodge for her faith in the project.

Last, but by no means least, I would like to thank my partner Helen; my family and friends, and my clients and customers.

John Such 2006
suchgoodpictures.co.uk

Published in 2006 by
Alison Hodge
2 Clarence Place, Penzance, Cornwall TR18 2QA
info@alison-hodge.co.uk www.alison-hodge.co.uk

Reprinted 2006, 2008

Photographs © John Such 2006
Introduction © Liz Luck 2006
This edition © Alison Hodge 2006

British Library Cataloguing-in-Publication Data
A catalogue record for this book is available from the British Library.

ISBN 13 978 0 906720 49 3
ISBN 10 0 906720 49 4

Cover designed by Christopher Laughton
Book designed and originated by
BDP – Book Development and Production, Penzance, Cornwall
Printed in China